LOAN EXHIBITION

C. Pissarro.

Under the patronage of
Monsieur Michel Legendre,
Consul General of France in New York and
Monsieur Edouard Morot-Sir,
Cultural Counselor to the French Embassy

For the benefit of
Recording for the Blind, Inc.

March 25th to May 1st, 1965

Wildenstein

19 East 64th Street, New York

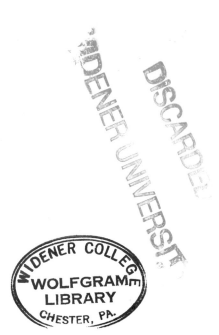

THIS EXHIBITION HAS BEEN MADE POSSIBLE THROUGH THE GENEROSITY OF THE FOLLOWING:

(Continued)

We extend our grateful appreciation to Mrs. Frederick B. Payne, Chairman, Mrs. Mario Pansa, Vice Chairman and to all members of the Art Committee responsible for the success of this exhibition.

We express our sincerest thanks to Dr. John Rewald for contributing the foreword to the catalogue.

Color plates courtesy Harry N. Abrams, Inc.

RECORDING FOR THE BLIND, INC.

Here in New York and in 15 cities across the country, 2400 trained volunteers are recording books—not just any books, but textbooks requested by some 3500 blind students in school, college or adult education. On the average, these students will do better than students with sight; some of them will become members of Phi Beta Kappa; most of them will achieve successful careers.

This year Recording for the Blind will record 2000 new titles in 12,000 copies. From its Library of 50,000 recorded books—the largest collection of its kind in the world—we shall distribute 25,000 books free on loan.

"Instead of pitying us, you give us the tools to help ourselves," one student said. "That's why Recording for the Blind is such a blessing."

The admission you paid for this exhibit will help more blind students to achieve independent and productive lives.

CAMILLE PISSARRO

PISSARRO, unlike van Gogh, was anything but an impulsive creator. The restfulness and mildness that characterized Camille Pissarro as a person, qualities he had in common with Corot, did not desert him during his work, to which he daily devoted a specific span of time. A man of deep convictions, of tremendous devotion to his calling, and of an enormous zeal, he knew of course that it is not possible to create masterpieces day in and day out. True artist that he was, he knew that the masterpiece is not brought about by waiting for a moment of divine revelation; he knew that it is achieved through constant work alone. Thus he endeavored to spend regular hours in front of his easel—either out in the fields, on country roads, at the market place, or in his studio—although his efforts were frequently hampered by the concerns that a large family and a small income cause. It can not always have been easy to work in the midst of all the worries occasioned by the absence of funds, by the bitter feelings of an exhausted wife, by the illness, and even death, of children.

It may seem trite to point out his difficulties, but it is an unfortunate fact that Pissarro wasted a great deal of his energy on the struggle for existence. Compared with him, van Gogh seems carefree, because he at least had a small monthly allowance from his brother which provided a certain minimum. Pissarro and his family of seven heads were often faced with nothing. It is useless to speculate on the amount of work he might have done had he not been forced monthly to lay down his brushes, journey to Paris and go from one collector and dealer to the other, often returning home without a penny. In view of the dire need he faced for decades, his work must be considered a marvel.

His battle was not confined to material difficulties alone. He had also to struggle with the problems set by his art, and thus had to contend with the capriciousness of nature, the changes of light, the transformations created by a sudden shower, the instability of a sky from which an unexpected wind chased picturesque clouds. No day ever resembled the preceding one, and although Pissarro went about his work with great regularity, there was no room for routine in his approach to his paintings. Each day and each canvas presented a challenge that had to be met on its own terms. There were days when he labored painfully but found it impossible to achieve the desired result; there were others when he thought to have caught the hoped-for effect, only to realize that somewhere something had gone amiss; and there were others still, when everything seemed to flow with ease, until the sun set before he had completed a painting that could not be continued the following day.

That in spite of pressing cares and frustrations, in spite of adverse criticism and deep sorrows, Pissarro was able to devote himself so completely to his creations is one of the most moving aspects of his life. But this would be merely touching were it not that his achievements place him in the front rank of the Impressionists. His importance is increased by the undeniable influence he exerted over some of his friends, which made him, who was ten years older than most of them, something like the "Father of Impressionism."

Pissarro's early works reveal an influence of Corot, to which he soon added the vigor of Courbet's example and palette-knife technique. Yet it did not take him long to develop a personality that was strong enough to withstand the expressions of his chosen masters. His colors became steadily lighter; by 1865 he had banned black, bitumen, sienna-brown, and ocher from his palette. Cézanne subsequently said that at that time Pissarro advised him to use the three basic colors and their direct varieties only.

Since 1859—when he was twenty-nine years old—Pissarro had attempted with more or less success to show his paintings at the Salon. In 1863 he participated with Manet, Jongkind, Whistler, and many others in the historic Salon des Refusés. Five years later he submitted to the Salon jury a landscape that had been painted entirely out in the open. At the same time he tried to persuade his friends, particularly Cézanne and Guillaumin, likewise to work directly from nature. Pissarro was not one of those who keep careful watch over the things they discover; he was, on the contrary, always pleased to share with others what he had found. Deeply convinced that knowledge acquired by the individual belongs to the community, Pissarro all his life generously transmitted his experience to those who wished to benefit from it.

The Franco-Prussian war of 1870 drove the artist from Louveciennes, near Paris, where he had lived for some time. The invading Prussians destroyed many of the paintings Pissarro had to leave behind when he and his family fled to London. There he met Paul Durand-Ruel who bought two of his canvases, thus becoming not only Pissarro's dealer but, eventually, the dealer also of all Pissarro's friends, to the extent that from then on Durand-Ruel's fate was to be intimately linked with the artists first ridiculed and later admired as "impressionists."

Though he worked a good deal in London where he also met Monet, with whom he studied the British landscapists in the museums, Pissarro was happy to return to France at the end of hostilities. In the summer of 1871 he settled in Pontoise where he was to remain for the next ten years and to gather a circle of close friends. Cézanne repeatedly came to stay with him; under Pissarro's influence he learned to study nature more patiently and even copied one of Pissarro's landscapes in order to appropriate more completely his master's technique. Pissarro's works of this period are distinguished by great delicacy of observation coupled with firmness of execution, as well as by an indescribable confidence and freshness that appear to have been extremely contagious.

These were also the years of the first Impressionist group exhibitions, which were initiated by Monet but in which Pissarro was to play a decisive role and which earned him his share of invectives. Notwithstanding the fact that the various Impressionists held many basic concepts in common, each of them made his own contribution to the new style of which they became the proponents. While primarily interested in landscape — as were also Sisley and Monet — Pissarro liked to introduce into these human beings and animals which often become important parts of the composition. In this sense he was somewhat akin to Millet, except that his peasants in the field, his country lanes with horse-drawn wagons, his market scenes, dairy maids, or duckponds lack that particular sentimental element which Millet so frequently stressed. Indeed, it was the unsentimental and unliterary character, the unsophisticated approach, the originality of perception and complete absence of any pretense that prevented Pissarro's work from finding favor with the general public.

One of the few collectors who showed interest in Pissarro was a bank employee, Paul Gauguin, who, after acquiring a small collection of Impressionist canvases, turned to Pissarro for advice when he decided to become a painter himself. During several years he closely followed his mentor. Although their friendship was eventually clouded by misunderstandings and disagreements, Gauguin still remembered Pissarro on his South Sea island and shortly before his death wrote: "He was one of my masters and I do not deny him."

In the eighties, Pissarro moved from Pontoise to nearby Osny and thence to Eragny, a small village much farther from Paris. In 1885, at a time when he was going through a crisis during which he was particularly dissatisfied with his own work, he met through Guillaumin first Signac and then Seurat. Fascinated with their attempts to replace the intuitive perceptions of the Impressionists by a scientific study of nature's phenomena and by a "divisionist" technique based on optical laws, Pissarro, though in his middle fifties, did not hesitate to follow the two innovators, who were young enough to be his sons. The following year he passed on the new concepts to Vincent van Gogh who had just arrived in Paris and was anxious to become acquainted with the most recent developments in art. Yet when Pissarro himself, after a few years, felt that the unyielding rules of Seurat's theories imposed too many restrictions upon his vision and execution, he abandoned divisionism and returned to his more spontaneous technique. But the lightness and purity of color acquired during his divisionist phase remained, and actually constitutes the particular attraction of his subsequent work.

In the last years of his life, eye trouble caused the artist such difficulties when he painted in the open that he was forced to work in his studio or from behind closed windows. When the view from his house at Eragny ceased to reveal anything new, he migrated to Paris, where he frequently changed his domicile so as to paint several series of various aspects of the town as perceived from his apartments. Many of these late pictures are among his best and make a worthy finale to his long and eventful career. Nothing betrays the aging and suffering artist or the man who had known need and scorn for tens of years. Everything is fresh, brushed so superbly and felt with such enthusiasm, such optimism, and youthfulness that it inspires admiration.

When Pissarro died in the autumn of 1903, he had felt the first signs of a coming fame and had known the first indications of a modest but steady income. Among all his friends and colleagues, Pissarro, who never pushed himself to the front and who longed for nothing except to live for his work and to be able to create undisturbed, was one of the last to gain public recognition. Yet those who had known him and learned from him knew how to evaluate him even before the prices for his pictures began to soar. Not only did Gauguin recognize him as his master, but in 1906, the year in which he died, Cézanne, at sixty-seven, venerated by the young generation of artists, remembered an old debt with gratitude and had himself listed in the catalogue of an exhibition in his hometown of Aix: "Paul Cézanne, pupil of Pissarro."

JOHN REWALD

CATALOGUE

··· 1 • *La Route*, ca. 1864
13¾ x 10¼ inches
P. & V. No. 35*
Lent by Dr. and Mrs. Gordon Pollock

*"P. & V." refers to LUDOVIC RODO PISSARRO ET LIONELLO VENTURI:
Camille Pissarro, Son Art — Son Oeuvre, Paris, 1939.
Unless specified, all paintings are oils on canvas.

— 2 • *Bords de la Marne en Hiver*, 1866
36⅛ x 59⅛ inches
P. & V. No. 47
Lent by The Art Institute of Chicago
(Mr. and Mrs. Lewis L. Coburn Fund)

~ 4 • *La Sente de la Justice, Pontoise*, 1869-70
20½ x 32 inches
Lent by Mr. and Mrs Hugo Dixon

5 • *La Route de Saint-Germain à Louveciennes*, 1870
15¼ x 18¼ inches
P. & V. No. 74
Lent by Mr. Sam Salz

6 • *Lower Norwood, London*, 1871
15¾ x 19¾ inches
P. & V. No. 112
Lent by Mr. and Mrs. Edward McC. Blair

7 • *Le Village de Voisins,* 1872
18¼ x 21¾ inches
P. & V. No. 139
Lent Anonymously

8 • *La Route de Rocquencourt,* 1871   *more subdued colors*
20¼ x 30½ inches
P. & V. No. 118
Lent by Mrs. M. Pereire

9 • *Chataigniers à Louveciennes, 1872*
16⅛ x 21¼ inches
P. & V. No. 146
Lent by Mr. and Mrs. Alex M. Lewyt

➝ 10 • *Paysage avec Petit Cours d'Eau, 1872*
18¾ x 22¼ inches
P. & V. No. 155
Lent by Mr. and Mrs. Jerome K. Ohrbach

11 • *Paysage avec Cheval Blanc dans un Pré, l'Hermitage*, 1872
18³⁄₁₆ x 21¾ inches
P. & V. No. 164
Lent by Mr. and Mrs. William Lasdon

12 • *Le Marché de la Saint-Martin, Pontoise, 1872*
21¼ x 25½ inches
P. & V. No. 178
Lent Anonymously

13 • *Rue à Pontoise*, 1872
18¼ x 21¾ inches
P. & V. No. 173

14 • *La Maison dans le Bois, 1872*
19¾ x 25½ inches
P. & V. No. 181
Lent Anonymously

15 • *Jeanne Pissarro Tenant des Fleurs*, 1872
28½ x 23½ inches
P. & V. No. 193
Lent by the Honorable and Mrs. John Hay Whitney

— 16 • *Le Jardin de Pontoise*, 1872
21½ x 25¾ inches
Lent by Mr. and Mrs. Grover A. Magnin

17 • *Portrait de Minette,* ca. 1872
18⅛ x 14 inches
P. & V. No. 197
Lent by the Wadsworth Atheneum, Hartford, Conn.

18 • *Bouquet de Roses*, ca. 1873
21⅝ x 18⅛ inches
P. & V. No. 198
Lent by Mr. Edwin C. Vogel

19 • *Le Tribunal de Pontoise,* 1873
13 x 16¼ inches
P. & V. No. 211
Lent by Mr. Peter A. Salm

~ 20 • *Usine près de Pontoise*, 1873
18⅜ x 22 inches
P. & V. No. 215
Lent by the Museum of Fine Arts, Springfield, Mass.

~ 21 • *Rue de Village, Auvers-sur-Oise,* 1873
21¼ x 26 inches
P. & V. No. 229
Lent by Mr. and Mrs. Guy M. Bjorkman

~ 22 • *Le Pont du Chemin de Fer, Pontoise,* ca. 1873
19½ x 25½ inches
P. & V. No. 234
Lent by Mr. and Mrs. David M. Heyman

~ 23 • *Effet de Neige à l'Hermitage, Pontoise,* 1874
21½ x 25¾ inches
P. & V. No. 238
Lent Anonymously

— 24 • *Effet de Neige à l'Hermitage, Pontoise, 1874*
21¼ x 25½ inches
P. & V. No. 240
Lent by the Fogg Art Museum, Harvard University,
Cambridge, Mass.
(Gift of Mr. and Mrs. Joseph Pulitzer, Jr.)

25 • *La Route à Ennery*, 1874
21¾ x 32 inches
P. & V. No. 255
Lent by the Museum of Fine Arts, Boston

26 • *Le Jardin de la Ville, Pontoise*, 1874
23⅝ x 28¾ inches
P. & V. No. 257
Lent by Mr. and Mrs. Arthur Murray

27 • *Gardeuse de Vache sur la Route du Chou, Pontoise*, 1874
21¾ x 36½ inches
P. & V. No. 260
Lent by Mrs. Edna H. Sachs

28 • *Rue de l'Hermitage, Pontoise, 1874*
16⅛ x 12¾ inches
P. & V. No. 264
Lent by Mr. and Mrs. Robert W. Sarnoff

29 • *Effet de Neige à Montfoucault, 1874*
16 x 20 inches
P. & V. No. 286
Lent by Mr. and Mrs. Lester Avnet

30 • *Le Chemin Montant, l'Hermitage, Pontoise,* 1875
21¼ x 25¾ inches
P. & V. No. 308
Lent by The Brooklyn Museum

31 • *Paysage à l'Hermitage, Pontoise,* 1875
21¼ x 25¾ inches
P. & V. No. 335
Lent Anonymously

32 • *Vue de Saint-Ouen-l'Aumone,* 1876
21¾ x 36 inches
P. & V. No. 344
Lent by Mr. and Mrs. Frank Altschul

33 • *Le Jardin des Mathurins, Pontoise, 1876*
45 x 65 inches
P. & V. No. 349
Lent by the William Rockhill Nelson Gallery of Art,
Kansas City, Mo.

34 • *Bords de l'Oise, Pontoise,* 1877
15 x 21½ inches
P. & V. No. 403
Lent by Mrs. Herbert H. Lehman

~ 35 • *La Vieille Route d'Ennery à Pontoise, 1877*
36¼ x 59 inches
P. & V. No. 415
Lent Anonymously

36 • *Le Parc aux Charrettes, Pontoise, 1878*
25½ x 21 inches
P. & V. No. 442
Lent by Mr. and Mrs. Benjamin M. Reeves

37 • *Le Pont de Pontoise,* 1878
23¾ x 28¾ inches
P. & V. No. 443
Lent Anonymously

38 • *Paysage sous Bois à l'Hermitage, Pontoise*, 1878
18 x 22 inches
P. & V. No. 444
Lent by Mr. and Mrs. Andre Kostelanetz

– 39 • *Portrait d'Eugène Murer*, 1878 ~~Ul pechief~~
25⅝ x 21⅜ inches
P. & V. No. 469
Lent by the Museum of Fine Arts, Springfield, Mass.

~ 40 • *La Crête du Chou, Pontoise,* 1879
18⅛ x 21⅝ inches
Lent by the Lazarus Phillips Family Collection

41 • *La Femme à la Chèvre,* 1881
32¼ x 25½ inches
P. & V. No. 546
Lent by Mr. and Mrs. H. O. H. Frelinghuysen

42 • *Inondation à Pontoise*, 1882
21¼ x 25½ inches
P. & V. No. 557
Lent by Mr. and Mrs. H. O. H. Frelinghuysen

43 • *La Côte du Chou à Pontoise, 1882*
32 x 25⅝ inches
P. & V. No. 568
Lent by Wildenstein & Co.

44 • *Le Marché à la Volaille, Pontoise,* 1882
distemper and pastel, 31⅞ x 21½ inches
P. & V. No. 1361
Lent by Dr. Sonja Binkorst Kramarsky

45 • *Le Cours-la-Reine, Rouen, 1883*
21½ x 25½ inches
P. & V. No. 603
Lent by Mr. and Mrs. Paul M. Hirschland

46 • *Quai Napoléon à Rouen,* 1883
21¼ x 26 inches
P. & V. No. 606
Lent by Mr. and Mrs. William Coxe Wright

47 • *Pommier à Eragny*, 1884
18¼ x 21¾ inches
P. & V. No. 635
Lent Anonymously

48 • *Le Chemin de Fer de Dieppe, Eragny,* 1886 *pointillist*
21¼ x 25⅝ inches
P. & V. No. 694
Lent Anonymously

49 • *La Rue d'Eragny, Vue par la Fenêtre (Le Sorbier)*, 1887
21⅞ x 18 inches
P. & V. No. 714
Lent by Mr. and Mrs. Morris Sprayregen

50 • *La Cueillette des Pommes, Eragny*, 1888
23⅝ x 28¾ inches
P. & V. No. 726
Lent by the Dallas Museum of Fine Arts

~ 51 • *Le Marché de Gisors*, 1889
distemper, 20¼ x 24⅝ inches
P. & V. No. 1433
Lent by Mrs. Doris W. Vidor

52 • *Hampton Court Green*, 1891
20½ x 28 inches
P. & V. No. 746
Lent by Mrs. Mellon Bruce

53 • *Old Chelsea Bridge, London,* 1890
23½ x 28½ inches
Lent by Mr. and Mrs. John D. Rockefeller 3rd

54 • *Faneuses au Repos*, 1891
26 x 32⅛ inches
P. & V. No. 773
Lent by the McNay Art Institute, San Antonio, Texas

55 • *Le Marché aux Grains à Pontoise, 1893* *une colès*
18 x 15 inches
P. & V. No. 862
Lent by Mr. Martin Nachmann

56 • *Le Jardin au Printemps, Eragny,* 1894
21¼ x 25½ inches
P. & V. No. 879
Lent by Mr. and Mrs. George W. Headley

~ 57 • *Le Moulin de Knocke,* 1894-1902
25⅝ x 31⅞ inches
P. & V. No. 883
Lent by Mr. and Mrs. Simon Jaglom

— 58 • *Le Noyer et Pommiers en Fleurs, Eragny, 1895*
28¾ x 23⅝ inches
P. & V. No. 916
Lent by Mr. and Mrs. Charles V. Hickox

59 • *La Baigneuse dans le Bois*, 1895
23¾ x 28¾ inches
P. & V. No. 904
Lent by The Metropolitan Museum of Art,
The H. O. Havemeyer Collection, 1929.

— 60 • *Le Pont Boieldieu à Rouen,* 1896
28½ x 36 inches
P. & V. No. 948
Lent by The Art Gallery of Toronto

COLOR PLATE ON REVERSE SIDE:
61 • *Le Grand Pont, Rouen,* 1896
    29 x 36 inches
    P. & V. No. 956
    Lent by the Museum of Art, Carnegie Institute, Pittsburgh, Pa.

colors are different (not so much green)

62 • *Matin, Temps Gris, Rouen*, 1896
21¼ x 25¾ inches
P. & V. No. 964
Lent by Mr. Gregoire Tarnopol

— 63 • *Quai Saint-Sever, Rouen*, 1896
28¾ x 36¼ inches
P. & V. No. 970
Lent by Mr. Hal B. Wallis

– 64 • *Les Toits du Vieux Rouen, Temps Gris*, 1896
28½ x 36 inches
P. & V. No. 973
Lent by the Toledo Museum of Art

65 • *Boulevard Montmartre, Mardi-Gras*, 1897
25⅝ x 31⅞ inches
P. & V. No. 995
Lent by Mr. and Mrs. Henry R. Luce

66 • *Boulevard Montmartre, Printemps*, 1897
25⅝ x 31⅞ inches
P. & V. No. 991
Lent by Mr. and Mrs. John L. Loeb

67 • *L'Avenue de l'Opéra, Soleil du Matin,* 1898
25⅝ x 31⅞ inches
P. & V. No. 1025
Lent Anonymously

68 • *La Rue de l'Epicerie, Rouen*, 1898
31⅞ x 25⅝ inches
P. & V. No. 1036
Lent by The Metropolitan Museum of Art.
(Mr. and Mrs. Richard J. Bernhard Fund, 1960.)

69 • *Rouen, Effet de Brouillard, 1898*
25⅝ x 31⅞ inches
P. & V. No. 1040
Lent by a Private Collector, Switzerland

70 • *Le Port de Rouen,* 1898
25⅝ x 31⅞ inches
P. & V. No. 1054
Lent by The Montreal Museum of Fine Arts

71 • *Bouquet de Fleurs,* 1898
21¼ x 25¾ inches
P. & V. No. 1064
Lent by Mr. and Mrs. Marco F. Hellman

72 • *Portrait de l'Artiste,* ca. 1898
13¾ x 12½ inches
P. & V. No. 1114
Lent by Mr. Edwin C. Vogel

73 • *Meules de Foin dans le Pré, Eragny*, ca. 1899
28½ x 36 inches
P. & V. No. 1072
Lent by Mr. and Mrs. Sidney R. Rabb

74 • *Temps Gris, Matin, Eragny,* 1899
23¾ x 28¾ inches
P. & V. No. 1080
Lent by Mr. and Mrs. Robert E. Eisner

75 • *Le Jardin des Tuileries*, 1899
28¾ x 36½ inches
P. & V. No. 1097
Lent by Mrs. Marshall Field

76 • *Le Carrousel, Temps Gris,* 1899
21¼ x 25¾ inches
P. & V. No. 1109
Lent by Mr. Gregoire Tarnopol

77 • *Jeanne Lisant,* 1899
21½ x 25½ inches
P. & V. No. 1111
Lent by Mr. and Mrs. Daniel Maggin

78 • *Le Pont Neuf,* 1901
18 x 15¼ inches
P. & V. No. 1177
Lent by the Allen Memorial Art Museum, Oberlin College,
Oberlin, Ohio

79 • *Le Pont Neuf,* 1901
17¾ x 15 inches
P. & V. No. 1179
Lent by Mr. and Mrs. Joseph S. Gruss

80 • *Le Pont Neuf, Après-Midi, Soleil, ca.* 1901
28¾ x 36¼ inches
P. & V. No. 1181
Lent by Mr. and Mrs. William Coxe Wright

81 • *Les Bains de la Samaritaine, Après-Midi,* 1902
15 x 18 inches
P. & V. No. 1214
Lent Anonymously

82 • *Le Louvre, Vu du Pont Neuf, Hiver*, 1902
21¼ x 25⅝ inches
P. & V. No. 1221
Lent by The Josten Collection

83 • *Place Henri IV*, 1902
25½ x 21¼ inches
P. & V. No. 1225
Lent Anonymously

84 • *Place du Vert-Galant,* 1902
29 x 36 inches
P. & V. No. 1227
Lent by Mr. and Mrs. David Schwartz

85 • *Les Roses de Nice,* 1902
18¼ x 21¾ inches
P. & V. No. 1273
Lent by Wildenstein & Co.

86 • *La Seine à Paris, Pont Royal,* 1903
21½ x 25½ inches
P. & V. No. 1293
Lent by Mr. and Mrs. Daniel Maggin

87 • *Port du Havre*, 1903
23¼ x 32 inches
P. & V. No. 1305

ADDENDA

42B • *Les Jardins de l'Hermitage, Pontoise,* 1882
21¼ x 25½ inches
P. & V. No. 558
Lent by Mr. and Mrs. Horace C. Flanigan

54B • *Paysanne Assise et Paysanne Agenouillée,* 1893
18 x 21½ inches
P. & V. No. 858
Lent by Mr. and Mrs. Harry C. Cushing 4th